# The Perfect Mother

by the same author

*My Grandparents Were Married for Sixty-five Years*
*A Little Ignorance*  (a novel)
*These Are My Same Hands*

# The Perfect Mother

# Penelope Scambly Schott

*Snake Nation Press*
Valdosta  Georgia

1994

# Acknowledgements

Several of these poems have appeared or are forthcoming in the following journals: *American Writing, The American Voice, Antenna, Bloodroot, Blue Line, Blue Unicorn, Calliope, Caprice, Common Woman, Confluence, The Devil's Millhopper, Feminist Studies, Footwork, The Georgia Review, Iris, Ms., Poets On, Roberts Awards, Shenandoah, Slow Dancer, Southern Poetry Review, South Florida Poetry Review, The Sow's Ear, Stone Country, US 1 Worksheets, Weid, West Wind Review.*

Some were included in the following chapbooks: *My Grandparents Were Married for Sixty-Five Years* (Journal of New Jersey Poets, Fairleigh Dickinson University, 1977) and *These Are My Same Hands* (State Street Press, 1989).

And books: *I'm On My Way Running,* Lyn Reese, Jean Wilkinson, and Phyllis Sheon Koppelman (Avon Books, 1983); *Keener Sounds: Selected Poems from The Georgia Review,* eds. Stanley W. Lindberg and Stephen Corey (University of Georgia, 1987; *The Curse,* Janice Delaney, Mary Jane Lupton, and Emily Toth 1988); The State Street Reader, ed. Judith Kitchen (State Street Press, 1990); *Women of the Fourteenth Moon,* eds. Dena Taylor and Amber Coverdale Sumrall (Crossing Press, 1991).

"Girls Embracing Knowledge" the 1991 Cynthia Cahn Memorial Poetry Prize issued as a poster by Anhinga Press.

Also, many thanks to the New Jersey Council on the Arts for grants in 1981, 1984, and 1987.

Cover by Marshall Smith

Editors: Roberta George
Nancy Phillips

Sponsored by: The Georgia Council for the Arts
Porter Flemming Foundation

Snake Nation Press
110 #2 Wes Force
Valdosta Georgia 31601

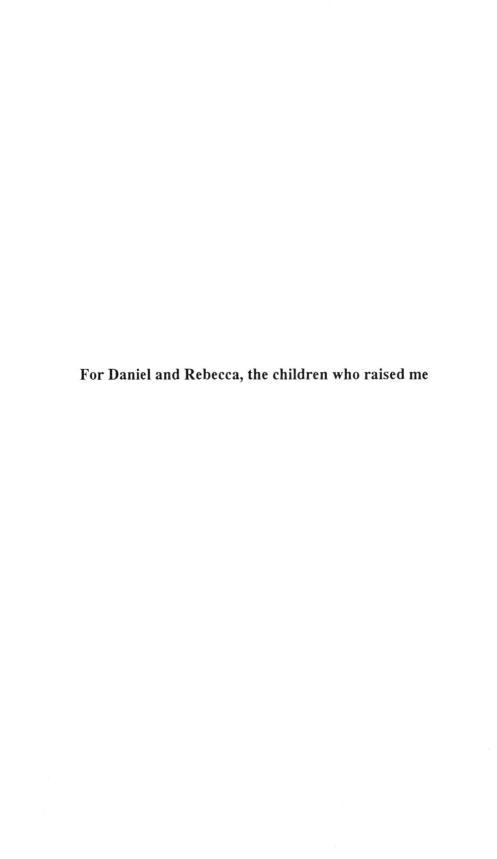

For Daniel and Rebecca, the children who raised me

# Contents

## 3. Girls Embracing Knowledge

# 1.  Blessed Are the Mothers

# Her Daughter's Neck

and the child bends her head
until the hair parts at the neck
and falls aside.  Nothing
the mother has touched or imagined
could crack more easily;
she believes she cannot bear it.
Her hands gifted with eyes
like the blind woman in the chapel,
she fingers the visible spine bone by bone
and over and over like rosary beads.
She has just one prayer:
*Look!* she points at the sky
all emptied of white birds,
and the child lifts her head.

# Everybody Else Calls Him Dan

My son and I
ride the long rim of the hill
where twilight is a violet line,

and I ask him,
*Is the moon full everywhere at once?*
What a dumb question

when what I really mean is
*Daniel, Daniel, Daniel.*
I press his hand in the dark

and let him go.
Of course he will see this same moon
over East Africa.

Pieces of sky lie below us.
Low, over the black quarry, below us,
the yellow moon is enormous.

# The Woman Who Went Backwards

The woman who went backwards did everything very well:
when her daughter's little breasts flattened to nipples,
when the brown hair fell off her son's lip,
she never even asked the pediatrician.

When the children reverted to superheroes
flailing about in purple towels,
when they pounded her French pots on the kitchen floor,
she withstood the noise and gave the right responses.

By the time they were both babies,
she was the perfect mother;
she always did the right thing,
as the right thing was whatever she did.

When the two children grew
red and wrinkled and wet and squeezed
themselves back up into her
(even—I should mention—in the right order),

she was very pleased;
except she was a trifle disconcerted
when the geese flew backwards
under the clear pond

and her eyes
contained nothing but sky.

# Blessed Are the Mothers

They say that
women
are too personal
we are not personal
enough

I am repeatedly overrun:
the migration of baby carriages,
the afternoon in the park.

Is he on solid foods now?
When did he sleep through the night?

Not: how to get the carriage up and down the curb
not: brown grocery bags squashing yellow blankets
not: the ache in the chest
        that drills
        and flattens, flattens you back
not: certainly not: the breasts
        which no longer
        which never did
        belong to you
When shall I sleep through the night?

My children are older now;
my hair, in good light, is turning white.
Sometimes, when I walk down the street,

I no longer register the steepness of curbstones.
I am now on solid ground.

The mothers are statues in the park:
I do not stop to read the inscriptions.
I am dressed with attention to color;
my accessories are chosen;
my children are in school.

I am not:   with a carriage
        :   with a carriage and a tricycle
        :   with a carriage and a tricycle and a dog
        :   with a carriage and a tricycle and a dog and
                                and heavy packages
I am:   with a man
   or:   on my way to meet a man
   or:   on my way to catch a bus
   or:   on my way to meet a woman
   or:   alone
From hips to knees to sidewalk, I am all motion.

The mothers are statues in the park:
I do not read the inscriptions.
I will not acknowledge:

The years you pay, over and over;
the long panic waking into the light;
my mother without a telephone,
myself without money, without friends,
the baby carriage on the elevator,
the soup pot on the stove,

the rain on the window,
        like bars.

This has nothing to do with love.

I looked up at my mother in the shower.
Then down. *Will I grow hair?*
I knew I would: I was only testing her.
*A little yellow fluff.*

In the eighth month I asked her, long distance
*It's nothing; you go to sleep*
            *and when you wake up*
            *you have a baby.*

I have already lied to my daughter.

They say that
women
are too personal
we are not personal
enough

# Blue Fear

Blue fear blooms
in my room.  Flinching

before a word.  My
mother calls me *Wrong.*

Consider those girls
whose names are promises:

*Grace, Hope, Felicity*—
their round hands enclosing

Sweetness, the gift
to please.  Six

years old and I know
what I know:  MY

hands are empty.

# Mommy Will Be Home in Time for Supper

Speeding back late down the turnpike
Rainbows of oil in swamp grass
Nothing at home for supper

But:  I bring gifts unto the children
Lo:  one all-beef salami
and Behold:  a box of real fortune cookies

*Love and travel await you*
May each day crunch in your teeth
We shall all be home in time

You will say you were waiting
First I waited for you
No man believes in his own birth

But the mothers remember the taste of pain:
Red blossom on a hard table
A pinched cookie pulled apart

# Nocturne for My Daughter

She, in pale flannel,
waves once and ascends,
her wristbone a white flute
whistling on the dark banister
curving upward and up
into the listening hall.

# Moving among Snow Women

She is so light she
does not break the smooth
skin of the snow. You
could almost mistake
her for juniper
by the porch step, she
lifts over such drifts
and treads so lightly
across your front porch.

Nobody hears her
but you, and you hear
her moving in your
house. Oh, she is not
loud in the warm blood
of radiators,
settling bones of old
boards. Not those noises.

No, I mean the dead
woman still palming
her white breadboard, soft
scuffs up the dark stair.

There, at the sharp turn
of the landing, you
can catch her, that shy

bride fingering her
veil.  Her damp hand stains
the rosewood newel
post, balances one
moment, and lets go.

Follow her down your
turning stairs.  Notice
how the light yellows
your parlor how each
February this
same astonishing
light hunts in corners

and you are bound up
in a long lace web.
The pattern of low
sun through these curtains
is a message your
own daughter will read
years and years from now
in another house.

# Goodmorning

### 1
Mama ups
my window.

Silver tree
says:
*Goodmorning,*
*little girl.*

I say,
*Goodmorning,*
*silver tree.*

### 2
Mama's face goes out in the dark
but when I call, Papa comes.  So
I don't call.

### 3
They think I fell.
I won't say how.
My brother knows.

Yes, my teeth bite
hard, and I would
too.

### 4
Papa says
Mama says
I should do

what Grandma says
until Mama
gets well.

  5
My sister
has no name
and very small fingers.

  6
Mother watches my new breasts.
*Almost summer*, she says,

and holds my sister under
the rounding moon.

  7
My brother doesn't think
I'm pretty.  Says he.
Who watches my window.

  8
Father says men tell lies.
He says you won't come.
Should I believe
him or you?

  9
When my sister
carried yellow
flowers today
she was almost
a butterfly
at my wedding.

10
Listen:  heart
under my heart.
Goodmorning,
little dawn.

11
The blood
in her hair is mine.
Nobody told me
ahead.

12
They dance her
  about a
    bout about;

Ten fingers
  and ten toes.
    If I cry now

13
or now:  how she,
in yellow grasses
down tumbling, grasps
my sister's knee.

14
I open her window.

Silver tree says:
*Goodmorning.*

I say:
*You forget*
*everything.*
*Please.*

## Back in Gretchen's Majestique Cake Shoppe
## My Mouth Wet with Possibility

Everything in that bakery
was just my height.
My big bossy mother
had to stoop, peer down
into cookies with chips
like sky has stars.

*Princess,* they called me,
beautiful in the bakery,
*Princess, would you like a cookie?*
And my mother, who always said no,
 said *yes.*

And every Friday shopping afternoon
I promised myself:
when I am big and rich like her,
then I will buy **two** gingerbread men:
one to keep alive
and one to bite off its head.

# Dream of a Woman Born in April

1
white
breast
red
mouth
blur

for
years
you
cry
out

2
in this one
she is 8
someone is
chasing her
terribly
round and round and
she dives

headfirst

under her
small white bed
and her head
of damp curls
does not crack

3
she
bears children
to mother
herself

4
you recall just
such a moment
where whatever
you most cherish
swallows whole
your unique bones

you intended
to go further,
*how sad,* you think,
*there was no time*

5
certain mornings
I understand
the soft broodings
of russet hens

6
offering:
in your backyard
succulent
green onion grass
cracks snowcrust
quick, quick, may some sweet mouth say quickly

what for thirst?
how to slake
this brooding
dream?

7
April rain tamps down the spaded grave:
in this one, she has died many times
and still does not know, even now,
that nothing has been accidental.

## Oh, Come to My Funeral, Mother,
## We Shall Dance on that Beautiful Shore

I am the daughter you always wanted
I won't embarrass you in front of friends
You can even shave my legs

Dust my children with your opinions
Maybe they'll stick
Play any music you like

The piccolo of coins
The double bass of money
I trust you

You'll be here for the taking-under
As you were there for my coming-out
It's all under control

A pile of dry leaves
I will never disappoint you again
My lapsing into flame

# They Love Us

They love us, those lonesome machines
from our childhood, cords frayed.

The iron fan exhales
our grandmother's plush rooms.

And this: the latticed toaster
(crumbs like sparrow eyes)

cries *feed me, feed me,*
flapping its brave gates.

# Rebecca Weeps, Collect

Nothing your Mama tells you
across rivers
suffices.

If
I die this morning,
they will find

me tangled in the frantic
ringlets of your hair.
If

you were a calf,
I would not suffer;
instead

my tongue would remember you
vaguely,
like thistle:

    silk spikes
    on purple velvet head.

# I've Forgotten My Name

I've forgotten my real name.
My two hands are not friends.
My feet float.  They tell me:
*You've been here already*
*and you didn't like it then.*
I surprise in the lens of my tears

my mother, as silver as ever.
When I brush her hand, the fingers
crumble.  I beg the knuckles:
*Can't we go home now?*  She says:
*This is your home.  Believe me.*
*Your only home.*

# 2. Woman in a Red Hat

# Poetry Reading: 1974

We are making much of our pain
Where there are two of us gathered together
it is among us
We are gathered here in celebration
My pain is at your service
Tell me, sisters, which shall it be tonight?

    the abortion at 15
    the suicide attempt
    the sadist
    the venture into child beating
    the first divorce
    the ones whose names I forget
    the custody suit
    the sheriff
    the mean drunk
    the state troopers
    the second divorce
    money
    no money
    other
    none of the above
    all of the above

Maybe you think I'm kidding?
God/dess forbid: these are my credentials.

It would, in this gathering, be rude to mention:

    two children like wild red poppies along a spring road
    or my grandmother's dark grape-stemmed silver
    or the long delicate back of a man
    all of which I
    shall, therefore, not mention
    in this company.

Ladies,
in tonight's rows
of folding chairs
the undoctrinal air
can never violate,
look
how each of my scars is uniquely beautiful,
crazed porcelain;
I am an *objet d'art*

and you will not get your money's worth
unless you see me crack.

# When I Was an Up-and-Coming Feminist Poet

1

When *Anger* was in,
I was officially angry
and almost famous.

I gave a good show,
snippy and smug.
As I rocked myself home on the bus,

I ranked
the *Seven Deadly Sins*
by preference:

*Gluttony*, thin as I was
who lived on free pickles
until my fingers bled,

or *Sloth*,
with extravagant yawn
who had no time to sleep.

In suburban living rooms
I *Envied*
the matched drapes I mocked.

Not *Lust*, though I always left
with my first choice
and felt nothing.

2
That *Pride* and *Shame*
are the same
sin,

I abased myself
to learn.  Years
later, I lay

down in the soybeans
among dry pods
and yellow flowers

and I screeched
from the depths
of my throat,

from the depths
of my raw
and celebratory throat,

my throat
full of old semen
and fury,

my lips
pursed with straight pins
and right answers,

my whole red mouth
with no song
in it.

# Thinking Now of American Poets

Left here, under the POSTED sign.  We're talking
    December; no flies.
South-east corner of my own woods.  The whole top of his
    skull
sliced off, so that before my brain could make a shape
out of that shape, before I could locate the word
*deer,* I was peering into a bloody bowl.

We're thinking now of American poets:
Nemerov with his goose fish; Stafford, his deer; even
    Gerald Stern
whose poems are otherwise completely thick and
    wonderful, and who was once
my friend, Jerry does it too, this sloppy insistence
on roadkill, the secret of life.

Such riotous disconnection, when any day in any town
a man could slather himself in gore—the curt E.R.'s
or the newly delivered, the translucent and membranous
    afterbirth.
But no, he runs it down with his pick-up or his car or
    simply happens
upon it, as a sign.

I could, if I chose, go one on one:
the groundhog so flat, the county painted the white
    line right
over it, or a thoroughly run-over skunk, its pelt

ground deep
into asphalt, its own white line.  But women drive the
    menstrual rag.

What do you use to slice a skull?
Do they carry hacksaws into the woods?
How do they cut the trophy antlers off?
What do you use to slice a skull?
What?

In medieval Europe, after every war, men organized
    *battues*
to kill the packs of wolves
grown numerous and fat on the field of battle,
twilight and dawn,
slipping out of the forest.

Eating.
Cleanly.

How can I walk in my own woods
where any thicket
holds a bloody bowl?

Take any mother's son, take mine:
he's twenty-eight and lives in Connecticut.
But wherever you find him, if you run him to earth,
if you kill him on bare ground, don't make the rain
do it, or invisible bugs in the guts of invisible bugs.

Do as the blessed cannibals do, who nourish flesh
with brother flesh.  Feed the earth to itself.
Twenty-eight years, and the sweet blue milk

drained from my breasts.
When you find him, punch your canines through the skin

into the pink-white meat. Glut your maw. Taste the warm
salt meat as it slides down the supple throat.  Let
   **that**
be your sign
of the world's goodness.

# The Poor Dead Feet of My First Husband

The smell crawls through the phone
as you speak your unspeakable news:
Disease, that eager bride,
has swamped you with dank embrace,
sucks all night at the stumps.

I see in this close air
how the slick knobs of your bones
in their separate cold pieces
lie wedged between wall and headboard,
each piece leaking.

My fingers splotch on the phone:
they will not touch again
that unresilient skin,
yellowy-white and shiny
like the fat on old meat.

In those years your damp flesh
lay on mine like a blight,
I moved away from my skin
and inside my fresh nightgown
I slept in a circle of air.

Somebody kind should gather
these small pieces of your death;
somebody kind should murmur
*How sad;* somebody kind,
somebody else.

# Custody

In the borough of Queens
where I lived then

I had driven all night on the boulevards
and had no hands.

I had traded her brother
for my life:

*You may take him,*
I promised. *Yes.*

It was Rumplestiltskin.
It was 1969.  I was still an idiot.

I dressed her in my shame
and took us to town:

in the sculpture garden
of the Modern

even Picasso's goat
could not console.

For many hours
we lived by ourselves

before her brother (in baseball pajamas)
was restored to us,

which partly explains
why my daughter is flesh

and my son
the remission of absence.

# HOW Do the Guilty Survive?

—for Ernest Kramer 1935-1984

1

HOW?  In the mouths of the innocent
who ignore me,

by the embraces of the wicked
who cherish me,

for the lust of the virtuous
who envy me.

What rots first:  OCULUS
or PHALLUS?


2

Of the full dozen men
I've squeezed in my nether hand,

yours is (I think) the only
penis deceased.

You gave me no pleasure.
I was too young and hated

my mother.
If you loved me, I'm sorry.

**44**

3

It was after Hiroshima,
it was before Pol Pot,

it was before Chernobyl,
it was 1968 but we had two kids

so I missed the show.
It was the night before

you left me;
I was so glad.

4

Afterwards, I was poor
and wanted symmetry:

I sat her with pigtails
in a ladderback chair;

her golden brother
has a slow leak in his soul.

How
do the Guilty survive?

5

For years, I took
anything I was offered:

a gallant came by with sickle pears
and yellow jackets for my tongue.

*Thank you,* I said.
*Thank you, for permission.*

Please carve on my tombstone:
SHE TRIED VERY HARD.


6

Both our children are adults.
I fed them and fed them.

When I finally had time
to look, nothing made sense;

I wanted to ask the birds:
*Why do you keep laying eggs?*

Our children wink
with your four brown eyes.

# And This

And this is the way I go to bed alone
singly or doubly, with him or only my own skin

for company, as I rub my feet against tucked sheets
in the safe pocket between day and night, and this

is the way my hands slip down the sharp bones
of the hips into the hollow between thighs, and this

is the way the heel of my hand presses the hair
under the sheet while clear up in my head

I total my bills, subtract my money, sort
my laundry, survey deadlines, reorder appointments,

inventory dust in the house, as I wait to float
up and up over the emptied bed

onto that high and narrowing ledge of sleep
before dreams.

# Landscape with Bottles

"LIVING WITH DRUNKS SOMEWHAT RESEMBLES
LIVING WITH VAMPIRES; IT GETS BAD AT NIGHT."

## 1. Fear of the Dark

After the curses
and large awkward fists
he will fall asleep
and look sweet, sleeping,

and you, you will sit
here at the window
in your torn nightgown
shivering all night.

You will discover
just before first dawn
how the neighbors' fence
offers its white light.

Accept this blessing.
Accept.  Close your eyes
to the dark street, now
you will go to sleep.

## 2. Conversation at 3 a.m.

At the kitchen table
I sip cold tea; this time
he wants to quit his job

and buy a lobster boat.
I keep sipping; only
the iron radiator
is not scared to object.


3.  He Is a Good Sleeper

When a grown man
wets your bed,

you bathe very quickly
and go downstairs;

you will wash bedclothes
in the morning.

This has happened before.
You regard him

and his long penis
with justifiable distaste.


4.  Out Here in November

The fit is on him:  he hunts
from room to room until

I fade like a wraith
out the back door

barefoot across the frozen lawn.
Between the garage

and thick old lilacs
I crouch, hoping

the small and chilly stars
will not illuminate

my white nightgown.

Through yellow window squares
he looks harmless

as any neighbor.
But what I notice most out here,

my cheek numb against lilac,
is how very easily

I could fall asleep.


5. Calling the Cops at Night

I speak
between my hands
into plastic,

talk fast
hearing his shoes
stumble up stairs.

Their car
drifts up the street
like a remote

lighthouse,
steady and clear
beyond the reef.


6. Carelessly

I forget
the loud sounds:
chairs cracking,
doors slammed shut

but am Oh!
startled by
the small song
of ice cubes.


7. Sainthood

*How did you stand it
for so many years?*

It wasn't easy.

*Then why didn't you
throw him out sooner?*

I liked being right.

# Woman in a Red Hat: 1975

I wore sharp elbows and a red beret,
I strode faster than anyone.

Every morning I put on my costume,
every night I took off my wrists.
It was a fun time.

I met Adrienne Rich and Betty Friedan,
I was good at that dance, whatever I was.

I should have been a she-bear
suckling my cublets in a cave.

My daughter ran off with my red hat
and returned, hatless.

I slapped her and slapped her.
No, I didn't.  I beat my head on the floor,

I hammered and hammered
on the red hot anvil of the floor.

# Feeding Angels

I think I know
what water dreams;

your face shivers
broken to foam.

If I go where
I've been, home is

another place.
When I light my

candle, angels
swoop.  I tell them:

*Eat. Eat.*  Incense
blooms in my palms.

Blessed be the moths,
these tiny moths,

these sugared moths,
my white daughters.

## When You Phoned Home from California
## to Tell Me It Had Started

A brilliant globule of blood
rolled out over the surface of the desert
up and down the Continental Divide
through the singing prairies
parting the Mississippi
leaping the Delaware Water Gap
until it spilled into this tall red kitchen
in Rocky Hill, New Jersey
where it skittered across the linoleum
and cracked into hundreds of little faceted
    jewels

I will not diminish this day with labeling
I will not say foolishly
*now you are a woman*
I will never tell you
*don't talk to strangers*

because we are each of us strangers
one to another
mysterious in our bodies,
the connections between us
ascending like separate stone wells
from the same dark waters
under the earth

But tonight you delight me like a lover
so that my thigh muscles twitch
and the nipples of my breasts
rise and remember
your small mouth

until I am laughing to the marrow of my bones
and I want to shout
*Bless you, my daughter, bless you, bless you;*
*I have created the world in thirteen years*
*and it is good*

# The New Life
### —for Eric

1. Thirsts

In the old life
I waited my turn:

I stood at the well
with my pitcher;

my tongue swelled black.
When I tell you this,

you don't vanish.


2. Grammar lesson

The most dangerous pronoun
in the whole stable of wild horses
is the word: *WE*

(as in *you* and *she*
as in *he* and *I*)

Let's see every movie in town
together;

let's stockpile *WE's*.

3. Double feature

Our knees
have a mind of their own.

We don't need the usher
pointing his flashlight:

the lantern in the belly
throbs like a lighthouse.


4. Stopping on the Interstate

When you took my griefs
in your arms
and rocked them all night,

I wanted to die.
I wanted to kiss your thumb.


5. The last circle

I may never
love you enough.

*I'm very patient,*
you say. *I'll wait.*

6. Wild white roses at dawn

From the yellow center
of the white blossom

I can walk toward you
in palest nakedness;

I can settle onto your skin
like petals into slow water,

a veil woven in water.


7. Leaves blow inside out before they taste of rain

The Grandmothers shake their silvered heads
and point a single skinny finger up:

*Beware the cat*
*who steals in the dark*
*the child's milky breath.*

But I, in clearest morning, know
so many lovely uses for my tongue:

Beware the poet;
she'll tell every-
body about

your body.

8. Laying the walk

At 90 degrees in the bare sun
your back shines.

I step from the cool house
bearing in hand

your glass of water,
as if from a temple.

The well descends 300 feet
and tastes of earth.


9. Nest

A pair of plain birds
nest in the open soffit
above our rain gutter.

Let's not slam doors
or screen the soffits;
let's buy a field guide

and walk out after supper
and baptize these birds.
*You are:*

## 10. The Dig

I imagine these two gold rings
under windless dirt:

after there's nothing
but knuckle,

our two left hands
struck apart by shovel;

and bedazzled about us,
the young and clustered scholars.

# 3. Girls Embracing Knowledge

# Every Minute

Every minute is like waking
from a dream where this gold ring
spins between red knuckles,
the diamond shining through
soapy water.  I've scrubbed
this same pitcher twenty
years.  Though how I came

to stand in this kitchen
tonight is a mystery
like children or strangers
gone out of my bed.
Only the full moon, great
white eye at the window, looks
familiar.  Just as

I step through the wall,
the whole sky spins round
and around, trailing
a wind like falling down, and
chipping off years as I fall.
When I was a child, there were
more stars.  This little

light arrives from a far place.
Down it floats, rustling silken
bells.  It soaks me in invisible
color.  Light gathers itself
into the palms of my hands

where it cannot mind
how I've been broken.

# The Rock of this Odd Coincidence

How these old hills flow down
beneath houses and roads and supermarkets,
down into the pool of evening,

only a small chip of a moon rising.

It will not do to speak of cities
nor how the flat cement
is crowding my grandfather's bones
in a square of sour dirt.

He said he remembered the Indian wars
and the edges of Chicago all cornfields.

Not on the trolley or the El'
shrieking sparks in the night,
not in my grandfather's Model-T's
or even the Packard I almost remember,
nobody goes back.

In the thin moonlight
I know how the heat of our star
is all spinning away:
the tidy woodpile scalloped in snow,
the diamond-faceted coal,
my own breath steaming.

To ask for reasons
merely presupposes reasons
here on this rock of odd coincidence
where none of us, no, not one,
asked for these lives.

# The Reconcilements of Elk Lake

### 1
Tonight Elk Lake is crammed
with stars.  From up in the thick disk

of the Milky Way, I am spying
on myself

head
down

in the outer suburbs
of an ordinary galaxy.


### 2
Nothing I hear
is unimaginable:

that a woman could strangle her baby
—whom she loves—makes perfect sense,

or the end of the world
come upon us, one way or another.

Only my kids in their omnipotent twenties
say, *Not in my time.*

3
SUNRISE MOUNTAIN, the trail map calls
this wooded hill: birch and pine and

my thin, thin mother
climbing

gently, though Daddy
with his mended heart

is breath-
less.


4
What I want to ask them both
about being old, is

*How do you plan?*


5
When I was a child, I drew these same
tiny islands

beside make-believe continents.  You see,
I still expected

to be surprised.

6

In the old movie house, the chandelier
like a great Foucault pendulum

swings
to the roll of the earth.

The movie never repeats
exactly.  As the universe

widens, we are farther and farther
apart and reaching

back into the
exploded center.

# Nothing is Moving

Nothing is moving on this last day of the year.  Even the
    titmice
have left the feeder.  The canal has frozen all the way
    across.
Beneath the ice the water flows but I don't believe it,
just as I didn't believe any young man in the airport
would turn out to be my son.

What I'm talking about is the diminishment of
    probabilities
so that when he is not in the first wave of passengers, or
    the second,
and when I don't see his shoulders riding down the
    escalator,
it seems less and less likely he will appear at all.

In the school auditorium I used to pretend, *Which child
    is mine?*
and I rested my love on one dark head after another,
until sound like a beam from his wide, unmistakable mouth
drew me up to the stage.

The year he spent abroad, I stared into the exact absence
    of his voice,
hearing among the large, ungainly boys, in all their
    brittle *glorias*
the hole his perfect baritone should fill.

Last week in the airport, he could have been anyone,
the guy in the hat, or the guy with his jacket hooked on
    his thumb,
or even the man with the stroller, helping someone, maybe.
Any youngish man in denim.  There, among strangers,
I almost believed in Schrodinger's cat:  half Daniel, half
    not.

I am always surprised when he arrives with his same face
    under his face
because, you see, there's this other son, the fictional
    son, who phones on Sundays.
Right here in my kitchen, he makes me shy.  I want to cook
    small goodies;
*You used to like this,* I want to say.

Oh, I once knew a high-bellied girl who counted down the
    days.
As she drew closer and then farther from her due date, she
    stopped believing
he would ever be born.

Listen:  the ice unzips like a zipper.  Each crack is like a
    pistol shot.
I can't say what it's like to be somebody's mother,
    somebody you sort of don't know.
It's easier to talk about the canal and how sometimes the
    cracks
will heal themselves so we may safely skate.

# Girls Embracing Knowledge

### 1

You too have seen them:
stacks of schoolbooks cradled to their chests.
From cinched waist to hunched shoulders,
they are all books: books lie on their breasts.

But their legs, like the legs of tall birds,
kick stones at the end of the drive.
They are not waiting for the school bus.
They are waiting for their real lives.

### 2

My pet, it will pull up in front of you
all right, when you are thirty-plus
or forty, and you will climb on board,
and your mom will be driving the bus,

and you'll know by the back of her neck
that whatever you did, or not, or error you
   embraced,
the years must still, unfailingly, deliver you
to this same place

### 3

a bright and unaccustomed yellow space
where gravity itself does not obtain,
nor time—something your textbooks
never could explain—a place

where you unfold your arms and drop
your heavy books, and lift
your little girl dressed up
for school

and cup your suckled breasts
and feel them rising up for hope,
for truant hope—
that sweet, uneducable fool.

# The Women We Have Become

### 1

We see in the old photos
the women we have become

even before the bones
fused, we practiced these faces

a child scowls into the Brownie
creasing, briefly, her forehead


### 2

After years of indifference
we recommence the count:

bleeding excessively or not
at all, or late enough

that the flicker of wonder
stuns us


### 3

We are become an embarrassment
to our children:  too female

for our large sons, smelling
(as we *do*) of the waters of life,

while our fierce daughters
(yes, even *you*) exact from us

nothing
we can spare

# Blue Veils

This blue-blue sun
and blind hooves
in the threshing yard:

I could have been
a man or a woman
or an ox.  The lowest

is a woman.
Kohl
blacks my eyes.

When I came to the well
I was walking
in somebody's life.

For 10,000 years
I have carried that life
on my head:

*water water*
*sticks and straw*
*the sticks  the straw*

Bury me now
by the stone well
among wide-haunched

cattle and the indigo voices
of mothers,
inside the water.

# Narcissus

To skip
across water
like a flat stone
flicked from the wrist:

only
an angry man
or a seeksorrow
resists such grace.

See how
the willow tips
finger their own
slender shadows;

how here
among lilies
and stumps, circles
swallow themselves;

how deep
in flat water
stares this woman
who skips lightly

as stone.

# Lost River Junction

### 1

We bob in the canoe
through the rapids of our birth,

later we think
we are paddling,

some of us
capsize—

some
of us—

even before the river
drops into the cave.

This keeps happening
though I can't tell it

to the big sons
with their snazzy

jobs, and their new
gray hairs.

### 2

*So-and-so,*
*beloved blip of bleep,*

*donations may be sent to:*
of what?  and how old?

My uncle is a boy
under the waves:

handsome arms, flung
across beautiful shoulders—

it's 1945
and everyone is smiling

as the ship goes down,
as every October

my mother
closes the door.

My father is forgetting
to sign his name.


            3
To say to the moment
*du bist, du bist*

so beautiful—
the sugar maple

again.  Each season
I get younger—

nothing surprises;
all astounds:

the mushroom spores,
the goldfinches becoming

potted chrysanthemums,
yellow, yellow,

or yellow itself
for which we evolved

our human eye.

# On the Edge of Visible Light

Out in a country past harvest
a woman stands perfectly still.
From the middle of a field
she reflects all colors, shines
clear white.  Her marble arms
bend with munificence.

Look how she carries mercy.
She lets me go and come back;
she lets me invent her.
In this land beyond violet
where invisible turns visible,
it is never too late.

*Mama,* I call across fences.
*Mama.  All this time, Mama,*
*in the dark furrows of my body,*
*in the willing flesh of my children,*
*I was asking for you.*

# Yellow Comb

### 1

What I wanted was I wanted
to wear my party shoes with straps.

Sniff each birthday. It's worse
than your mother told you. People
die of it.

### 2

What I want now
is to live like the frogs
whose souls are pure mud,

is to live like the chickens
whose souls are pure dirt.

### 3

The farm gone wild to scrubwood,
the chickenhouse fallen,

a pail full of holes,
this yellow comb to comb my hair.


4


Visit the old people
every week.  They are waxing their lips
with camphor.

Once they forget who you are, you are
your own mother.

Penelope Scambly Schott lives beside the Delaware and Raritan Canal
in Rocky Hill, New Jersey, with her third and final husband.

Her work has appeared in *The American Voice, The Georgia Review,
Lear's , Ms.,* and elsewhere, including a few anthologies.  She has
published a novel and two chapbooks of poetry and received fellow-
ships from the New Jersey Council on the Arts.  Her children have
triumphed over her imperfect mothering.